CONTENTS

INTRODUCTION

There are many ways to define an herb. In the botanical sense, an "herb" is an herbaceous plant that lacks a woody stem and dies to the ground each winter. Another definition describes herbs as any plant or plant part that has historically been used for culinary or fragrance purposes. And a broad definition of an herb is defined as a "useful plant" but one has to wonder what is meant by useful.

With a broad look at the word herb, it is possible to include hundreds of plants that fit the definition. While many herbs are in fact herbaceous, there are a lot that do develop woody stems. A gardener may wish to choose herb plants that have culinary value and aromatic value. And in addition to these traditional qualities, many herbs also offer a great deal of ornamental value to the garden as well.

Herbs can be classified as being either annual, perennial or biennial depending on whether they need to grow from seed each year or come back from overwintering crowns, roots, or bulbs. There are many herbs classified as tender perennials that are sold in parts of the country that do not allow them to overwinter successfully outdoors. These herbs are often grown in containers during the summer months and moved indoors before cold weather where they are overwintered in a sunny location of the home. Then next season they are moved back outdoors.

It is good to note the hardiness zones of the perennial herbs you buy and the hardiness zone where you garden. This helps to avoid disappointment thinking the herb you bought will be a permanent part of the garden when it may not be for the zone in which you are located. This necessitates planning on how you are going to overwinter the plant for next season.

Herbs can also be classified as either robust or fine (mild) herbs. Robust herbs are full bodied, rich in flavor and are often used alone or mixed with a few other herbs. Robust herbs stand up to cooking and may be used in dishes that are roasted, braised or grilled. Herbs such as rosemary, thyme, sage, and garlic would be classified as robust.

Fine herbs mix well with other herbs or when cooked, become milder. They are often added toward the end of the cooking process. Fine herbs are used in salads or eaten raw. Dill, basil, and parsley are considered mild and fine herbs.

CHAPTER ONE

What is Garden?

Garden, the laying out and care of a plot of ground devoted partially or wholly to the growing of plants such as flowers, herbs, or vegetables. Gardening can be considered both as an art, concerned with arranging plants harmoniously in their surroundings, and as a science, encompassing the principles and techniques of plant cultivation. Because plants are often grown in conditions markedly different from those of their natural environment, it is necessary to apply to their cultivation techniques derived from plant physiology, chemistry, and botany, modified by the experience of the planter. The basic principles involved in growing plants are the same in all parts of the world, but the practice naturally needs much adaptation to local conditions.

TYPES OF GARDENS

The domestic garden can assume almost any identity the owner wishes within the limits of climate, materials, and means. The size of the plot is one of the main factors, deciding not only the scope but also the kind of display and usage. Limits on space near urban centers, as well as the wish to spend less time on upkeep, have tended to make modern gardens ever smaller. Paradoxically, this happens at a time when the variety of plants and hybrids has never been wider. The wise small gardener avoids the temptations of this banquet. Some of the most attractive miniature schemes, such as those seen in Japan or in some Western patio gardens, are effectively based on an austere simplicity of design and content, with a handful of plants given room to find their proper identities.

In the medium- to large-sized garden, the tradition generally continues of dividing the area to serve various purposes: a main ornamental section to enhance the residence and provide vistas; walkways and seating areas for recreation; a vegetable plot; a children's play area; and features to catch the eye here and there. Because most gardens are mixed, the resulting style is a matter of emphasis rather than exclusive concentration on one aspect. It may be useful to review briefly the main garden types.

Flower gardens

Though flower gardens in different countries may vary in the types of plants that are grown, the basic planning and principles are nearly the same, whether the gardens are formal or informal. Trees and shrubs are the mainstay of a well-designed flower garden. These permanent features are usually planned first, and the spaces for herbaceous plants, annuals, and bulbs are arranged around them. The range of flowering trees and shrubs is enormous. It is important, however, that such plants be appropriate to the areas they will occupy when mature. Thus it is of little use to plant a forest tree that will grow 100 feet (30 meters) high and 50 feet across in a small suburban front garden 30 feet square, but a narrow flowering cherry or redbud tree would be quite suitable. Blending and contrast of color as well as of forms are important aspects to consider in planning a garden. The older type of herbaceous border was designed to give a maximum display of color in summer, but many gardeners now prefer to have flowers during the early spring as well, at the expense of some bare patches later. This is often done by planting early-flowering bulbs in groups toward the front. Mixed borders of flowering shrubs combined with herbaceous plants are also popular and do not require quite so much maintenance as the completely herbaceous border.

Groups of half-hardy annuals, which can withstand low night temperatures, may be planted at the end of spring to fill gaps left by the spring-flowering bulbs. The perpetual-flowering roses and some of the larger shrub roses look good toward the back of such a border, but the hybrid tea roses and the floribunda and polyantha roses are usually grown in separate rose beds or in a rose garden by themselves.

Woodland gardens

The informal woodland garden is the natural descendant of the shrubby "wilderness" of earlier times. The essence of the woodland garden is informality and naturalness. Paths curve rather than run straight and are of mulch or grass rather than pavement. Trees are thinned to allow enough light, particularly in the glades, but irregular groups may be left, and any mature tree of character can be a focal point. Plants are chosen largely from those that are woodlanders in their native countries: rhododendron, magnolia, piers, and maple among the trees and shrubs; lily, daffodil, and snowdrop among the bulbs; primrose, hellebore, St.-John's-wort, epimedium, and many others among the herbs.

Rock gardens

Rock gardens are designed to look as if they are a natural part of a rocky hillside or slope. If rocks are added, they are generally laid on their larger edges, as in natural strata. A few large boulders usually look better than a number of small rocks. In a well-designed rock garden, rocks are arranged so that there are various exposures for sun-tolerant plants such as rockroses and for shade-tolerant plants such as primulas, which often do better in a cool, north-facing aspect. Many smaller perennial plants are available for filling spaces in vertical cracks among the rock faces.

The main rocks from which rock gardens are constructed are sandstone and limestone. Sandstone, less irregular and pitted generally, looks more restful and natural, but certain plants, notably most of the dianthuses, do best in limestone. Granite is generally regarded as too hard and unsuitable for the rock garden because it weathers very slowly

Water gardens

The water garden represents one of the oldest forms of gardening. Egyptian records and pictures of cultivated water lilies date as far back as 2000 BCE. The Japanese have also made water gardens to their own particular and beautiful patterns for many centuries. Many have an ornamental lantern of stone in the center or perhaps a flat trellis roof of wisteria extending over the water. In Europe and North America, water gardens range from formal pools with rectangular or circular outline, sometimes with fountains in the center and often without plants or with just one or two water lilies (Nymphaea), to informal pools of irregular outline planted with water lilies and other water plants and surrounded by boggy or damp soil where moisture-tolerant plants can be grown. The pool must contain suitable oxygenating plants to keep the water clear and support any introduced fish. Most water plants, including even the large water lilies, do well in still water two to five feet deep. Temperate water lilies flower all day, but many of the tropical and subtropical ones open their flowers only in the evening. In temperate countries water gardens also can be made under glass, and the pools can be kept heated. In such cases, more tropical plants, such as the great Victoria Amazonia (V. regain) or the lotus (Nelumbo nucifera), can be grown together with papyrus reeds at the edge. The range of moisture-loving plants for damp places at the edge of the pool is great and includes many beautiful plants such as the candelabra primulas, calthas, irises, and osmunda ferns.

Herb and vegetable gardens

Most of the medieval gardens and the first botanical gardens were largely herb gardens containing plants used for medicinal purposes or herbs such as thyme, parsley, rosemary, fennel, marjoram, and dill for savouring foods. The term herb garden is usually used now to denote a garden of herbs used for cooking, and the medicinal aspect is rarely considered. Herb gardens need a sunny position, because the majority of the plants grown are native to warm, dry regions. The vegetable garden also requires an open and sunny location. Good cultivation and preparation of the ground are important for successful vegetable growing, and it is also desirable to practice a rotation of crops as in farming. The usual period of rotation for vegetables is three years; this also helps to prevent the carryover from season to season of certain pests and diseases.

The old French potager, the prized vegetable garden, was grown to be decorative as well as useful; the short rows with little hedges around and the high standard of cultivation represent a model of the art of vegetable growing. The elaborate parterre vegetable garden at the Château de Villandry is perhaps the finest example in Europe of a decorative vegetable garden.

WHAT IS AN HERB?

Herbs are defined as plants that are useful to humans. Not quite the same as a vegetable or a fruit, an herb is something we value for a variety of different reasons. An herb can be useful to us for its flavor, its scent, its medicinal properties or its use as an insecticide. Some herbs are used as coloring for dyes or for industrial uses. Herbs have been used for thousands of years in teas and balms to relieve physical ailments, such as upset stomachs and stress-induced illness. Herbs are not only useful to humans, but they are attractive as well. Gardeners use them as borders for their landscaping, along walkways, and mixed in with their flowers and shrubs. Cooks use them for the unique flavorings that they bring to food. Spices are plants that are used in many of the same ways as herbal plants but come from tropical regions. Spices are more difficult to grow. Herbs, on the other hand, can grow quite nicely almost anywhere that has a growing season. Herbs can be found as annuals (plants that live for one season), biennials (plants that live for two seasons), or perennials (plants that come back year after year).

COMMON HERBS

Chives (Allium schoenoprasum)

Lemon verbena (Aloysia triphylla)

Dill (Anethum grave lens)

Angelica (Angelica archangelica)

Chervil (Anthriscus cerefolium)

Horseradish (Armoracia rusticana)

Southernwood (Artemisia abrotanum)

Wormwood (Artemisia absinthe)

French Tarragon (Artemisia dracunculus)

Borage (Bora go officinalis)

Marigold (Calendula officinalis)

Caraway (Carum carvi)

Chamomile (Chamaemelum nobile)

Coriander (Coriandrum sativum)

Cumin (Cuminum cyminum)

Fennel (Foeniculum vulgare)

Woodruff (Galium odoratum)

Hyssop (Hyssopus officinalis)

Orris (Iris germanica florentina)

Bay (Laurus nobilis)

Lavender (Lavandula angustifolia)

Lovage (Levisticum officinale)

Lemon Balm (Melissa officinalis)

Mint (Mentha spicata)

Bergamot (Monarda didyma)

Sweet cicely (Myrrhis odorata)

Basil (Ocimum basilicum)

Marjoram (Origanum majorana)

Parsley (Petroselinum crispum)

Aniseed (Pimpinella anisum)

Rosemary (Rosmarinus officinalis)

Sorrel (Rumex acetosa)

Rue (Ruta graveolens)

Sage (Salvia officinalis)

Cotton lavender (Santolina chamaecyparissus)

Winter savory (Satureja montana)

Alecost (Tanacetum balsamita)

Feverfew (Tanacetum parthenium)

Common Thyme (Thymus vulgaris)

Oregano (Origanum vulgare)

WHY GROW HERBS?

Although they're loved by seasoned gardeners too, Hollie Newton – author of How to Grow – says herbs are a "beginner gardener's dream, because they're pretty much the easiest thing to grow."

It's better for your bank balance and the environment too. Growing your own parsley, rosemary or mint will mean you'll no longer have to buy those cellophane-wrapped fresh herbs from the supermarket, that tend to go bad after a few days causing wastage.

According to Guy Barter, Chief Horticulturist at the RHS, herbs are also great if you're short on space. "You can easily grow them on a sunny window sill or on a balcony," he says.

But the ease and simplicity of growing herbs isn't the only reason to get started. "As we're all becoming more aware of the environment and where our food comes from, there's something so interesting, satisfying and reassuring about cooking something you have grown," says Barter.For Newton, growing herbs – among other plants – also works wonders for her mental wellbeing. "I love gardening because you can't rush it – it takes its own time, and there's something really soothing about that in this world of speed and smartphones," she says. "Watching something grow from nothing is really magical."

WHAT KIND OF HERBS SHOULD I GROW?

You can try any you like! "I'd start with the dependable, everyday-cooking herbs, like basil, sage, coriander, mint and rosemary," Newton suggests. "But you can try out so many interesting varieties. I am currently growing Moroccan mint outside my back door, and lemon thyme which works amazingly with chicken. I also love growing chives, because the flowers are edible and they look great in salads."

WHERE CAN I GET THEM FROM?

Sadly, getting hold of seeds and plants from nurseries can be quite difficult at the moment, due to lockdown. But thankfully, Barter says there are ways around this. "There may be delays on orders, but while you wait for seeds to arrive, you can buy the pots of rosemary or basil from the supermarket, and transfer them into a different pot or bed at home, so you can nurture them and keep them growing," he recommends. "You can also buy big bags of coriander seeds from some shops and sow those – these can take around six weeks to grow but they still work really well."

WHEN SHOULD I GROW THEM?

Now is the perfect time, says Guy Barter. "The sooner you start, the better," he says. "If you start growing them in spring, they will grow well throughout the summer. Herbs like thyme, rosemary, lavender, sage and oregano are pretty hardy and will keep all winter."

What will I need?

Alongside your seeds or plants, you will also need pots – but according to Barter, these don't have to be anything fancy. "You can either use smaller pots to separate them, or one bigger, longer, pot," he says. "But if you don't have anything to hand, you can even use containers from the supermarket with holes in the bottom to ensure they have good drainage."

Then, you'll need to fill them with potting compost – although both Newton and Barter agree that if you can't get hold of any, some soil from the garden will work just fine.

"You don't need any other specialized equipment, except maybe a trowel would come in handy," says Barter. Just grab a watering can or spray bottle and you're all set.

CHAPTER TWO

What is an Herb Garden?

An herb garden is basically a garden that is being used solely to grow herbs. A better description of what an herb garden might be is a beautiful and relaxing place where you can find plants that are not only useful but beneficial to the enjoyment of life. An herb garden can be any size or shape and can contain many different types of herbs or just a few. An herb garden may take up an entire yard or may simply be planted in a small window box container. Herb gardens can be kept indoors on a sunny windowsill or outdoors in the open breeze. An herb garden design can also be incorporated into a vegetable garden, with landscape shrubbery, or mixed in with your flowers.

TYPES OF HERB GARDENS

There are many different types of herb gardens and many ways for using herb gardens, each with their own character and charisma.

Kitchen Herb Garden

A culinary, or kitchen, herb garden will consist of only herbs used for flavorings in cooking. Most are grown in containers, though they can be grown in the garden too, nearest the kitchen. It might contain:

Parsley

Basil

Chives

Oregano

Rosemary

Thyme

Fragrant Herb Garden

An aromatic herb garden will consist of herb plants that are highly noted for their fragrance and used for cut flowers, aromatherapy, or for making potpourri and scented candles. It might contain herbs like:

Lavender

Lemon balm

Scented geraniums

Herbal Tea Garden

An herbal tea garden will consist of herbs such as chamomile, anise, hyssop, and assorted mints that can be brewed into delicious teas.

Medicinal Herb Garden

A medicinal herb garden will consist of herbs used for soothing and comfort, where you might find aloe and feverfew. A word of caution on using herb gardens for medicinal purposes: while some herbs have been found to be helpful, other herbs can be harmful if ingested or used improperly. Always check with a doctor before starting any herbal remedy.

Ornamental Herb Garden

Ornamental herb gardens are prized for their beautiful flowers and unusual foliage. An ornamental herb garden might contain southernwood, sage, and germander. The most popular type of herb garden design consists of many different varieties of herbal plants, some for cooking, some for fragrance, some for beauty, and some for just soothing your soul. With so many wonderful herbs to choose from, the question shouldn't be what is an herb garden, but rather what is growing in your herb garden? If you're looking for some extra spice in your herb garden, consider adding exotic herbs to the garden. From Italian parsley, lime thyme, and lavender to allspice, marjoram and rosemary, there are endless possibilities for the exotic herb gardener. Exotic culinary herbs have been grown and cultivated throughout the world, from the Mediterranean to the Tropics, their versatility is unsurpassed. Exotic herbs are not only found in many places, but they have some amazing qualities, with many of them quite adaptable and easily grown indoors without little care. Let's learn a little more about exotic herb plants that you can grow in your garden.

TOOLS NEEDED FOR HERBS GARDEN

you'd be interested to know that this project is not as complicated as most would expect. In fact, I built my very own herb garden with the common hand tools that I use to repair furniture and fittings at home. Here is a list of tools that you will need:

Hand Saw: The handsaw is to be used for cutting pieces of wood to secure your garden or make props where needed.

Tape Measure: Use a tape measure to determine the dimensions of your garden.

Spade: This is the primary digging tool. You will need to dig the soil so that it becomes soft enough to plant your herbs.

Garden Fork: The fork loosens the soil by lifting and turning over the soil on your garden.

Drill and Screws: You will need to attach the parts of wood using screws. The drill creates holes for driving screws.

Trowel: The trowel breaks up the earth and digs small holes for which to plant herbs.

Watering Can: You will need to water your herbs regularly. A watering can do the job.

Screwdriver Bit Holder: Drivers screw into the holes in wood.

MATERIALS

Once you've gathered the necessary tools, you will also need the following materials:

Pre-cut wooden sleepers

Wood preserver to prevent the rotting of the wood

Coach screws

Soil

GARDEN DESIGN

Most herb roots get the majority of their nutrients from the top 6" of soil, so it's important to make that layer as rich and loose as you can.

Once the amendments have been worked into the soil, it's time to lay out the garden design. To break up the space and create the look of a low green wall, add some foundation plants. This will accomplish several things: First, it will help balance out any hard lines from walls or fences; second, it will give the area the look of an outdoor room; and third, it will give the garden some structure in the winter when the herbs die back.

Tea Olive

They are evergreen plants that get 6-10 feet tall and have flowers that smell like orange blossoms. Their dark green foliage will act as a backdrop for the herbs and the sweet smell will complement the stronger savory herbs.

Dwarf Boxwoods

They're a good choice because they keep their color year round and can be trimmed or clipped into almost any shape. A low hedge of boxwood never fails to look nice in an herb garden.

Lavender

There are many types of lavender, all of which can be sensitive to ground temperatures and the amount to moisture they get. Be sure to choose one that grows in your zone. Lavender forms a low-growing hedge that's full of purple flowers and fragrant branches in the spring and summer. Lavender is dried to use in soaps, perfumes and cooking. The flower heads are sold by weight; since they can be very pricey, growing your own is an inexpensive way to have a steady supply of this fragrant herb.

Rosemary

Its popularity makes it a must for any herb garden. Rosemary is easy to grow and will get very large if you don't trim it back every now and then; as it grows, you will need to keep it in a uniform shape. It's perfect for the corner where Joe is planting it, because it will add it some height and provide a backdrop for the smaller herbs he's putting in front of it. The upright look of the rosemary plants will provide a nice contrast to the looser structure of the annual herbs that will go in front of them.

These plants are all evergreen, and they're the only plants that will be green in the winter. It's very important that you pick plants that you like and that grow well in your area. If you don't think they look good now, or if they don't have the shape you want, you won't be happy with the garden later on. So be sure to do your homework and pick what's best for your taste.

Add some 10-10-10 slow-release fertilizer around the base of the plants and mix it in with the loose soil. This will help the plants get the nutrients they need to put out strong roots. This is especially important the first year until the plants get established. Finally, give all the shrubs a good drink of water. Always water new shrubs as soon as you get them in the ground; otherwise the surrounding dirt will soak up the moisture from the root ball and the plant will go into shock.

HOW TO START AN HERB GARDEN?

Gardening has been around for centuries as people have used it first and foremost as a food source and a means of livelihood. While those reasons are still prevalent today, many are getting into gardening as a hobby and as a way to be healthier and more economically responsible.

Herbs are able to add a lot of flavor to a variety of dishes and baked goods. You can also use them to brew your own tea. You can really enjoy whatever you make knowing it's all thanks to your green thumb!

Whether you're a novice gardener or just getting into it, starting an herb garden will bring you a lot of satisfaction without much hard work as herbs are able to grow in a variety of conditions. Use our detailed guide to learn how to start an herb garden.

Select the Herbs for Your Herb Garden

If you have a hankering for Caprese salads, basil is the gift that will keep on giving. And the same can be said for parsley, which like basil can be used as a flavorful addition to a number of dishes, but can also reign supreme in a big batch of pesto. (Pesto is my #1 reason for planting lots of basil and parsley – it freezes well and I like having it on hand all year round.)

If you're a pickling fanatic, don't skimp on the dill. You'll always wish you had planted more.

And if you love a fresh, oniony flavor on your veggies or in your breakfast omelets, plant yourself a nice supply of chives (blend it with butter for a great steak rub). Our chives come back more vigorously each year, so keep that in mind. Mint can be aggressive when it grows back the following season. It's great for drinks and some desserts, but I found myself clearing 50 sq. ft. of it from a neglected garden bed when I bought my house! And it kept coming back.

If salsas and guacamole are your specialty, plant some cilantro and be prepared for any friend and family get-togethers.

Both thyme and rosemary are powerful in scent and flavor, making them perfect additions to many recipes including meat and poultry, fish, in soups and on vegetables. Rosemary thrives easily year-round, but if you live in a colder zone, consider keeping it in a container that can move indoors during the winter.

Lavender is fun to grow yourself if you're into making homemade aromatics, or experimenting with it as a palate-cleansing flavor.

Lemongrass! For Southeast Asian dishes, and for those delicious green smoothies.

Once you decide you want to start an herb garden, you need to pick what herbs you'd like to grow in your herb garden. You can either start with seeds or starter plants, depending on your preference. There is a wide variety of herbs to choose from for your herb garden, including:

Basil

Chives

Mint

Coriander

Dill

Fennel

Tarragon

Parsley

Rosemary

Sage

Oregano

Thyme

Lemon balm

Lavender

There's a lot you can do with herbs. If you're looking to use them to cook with, basil, chives and oregano add a punch of flavor to savory dishes, while lavender and herbs like rosemary add both aroma and flavor to many baked goods. If you'd like to make tea or cocktails, mint is especially refreshing.

Choose Your Container for Growing Herbs

Once you decide what herbs you'd like, you need to find the right container for growing herbs. Even if you have space for a garden, or currently have a garden, planting your herbs in a container will be beneficial in many ways.

For one, herbs don't require much maintenance and planting them in a container allows you to move them indoors if and when the weather turns cold. You can also start your herbs in the winter or early spring and move them outdoors when the weather is ready for them.

Placing your growing herbs in individual containers is also aesthetically pleasing as you can put them in a variety of containers including:

Colored ceramic pots

Vases

Metal boxes

Wooden boxes

You can choose a bigger container and plant herbs with similar growing requirements together, if desired. However, you'll want to make sure to plant mint in its own pot as it tends to spread and can take over anything near it. Whatever container you decide on, it's important that it has drainage holes in order to avoid root rot. If not, you can simply drill a couple into the bottom of the container. It's also important to use high-quality potting soil.

The potting soil you plant your herbs in will be its foundation. If you think about it, the container and potting soil will be the home that nurtures your herbs so you'll want to choose a soil that gives herbs what they need to thrive.

Herbs will do best in a potting soil that holds water but also provides good drainage. One soil that we found does just that is Miracle-Grow Expand 'n Gro. Mix the soil thoroughly in a big container before using some to plant your herbs. A great thing about this mix is that it can be used whether you choose to plant your herbs in a container or in the ground.

Screw The Wood Blocks Together

Use the screwdriver bit holder to drive screws into the wood. It is easier if you have a powered drill that also has a screw bit holder. Ensure that the bolts are tightly fastened onto the screws so that your box stays firm.

Apply Wood Preserver

The wood preserver prevents rotting and insects boring into the wood. Use a painting brush to paint the inner and the outer sides of the structure that you have constructed. Always wear gloves when cutting and applying the preserver on the wood.

Pour Out the Soil Into Your Box Holder

I have chosen to plant my garden in a concrete yard. To prevent damaging the concrete surface, I lay a PVC paper before putting the soil. This way water and plant roots do not find their way into the concrete surface. Pour out the soil into the box' until it is full. Ensure that soil is free of pebbles and stumps that may hinder the development of the root structure of your herbs.

While it is not compulsory, you can improve the quality of the soil by mixing the soil with the compost matter. The compost matter can be bought from an agrovet (a place where farmers can purchase agricultural and veterinary products) or created using grass cutting after mowing.

Water Your Garden

The soil will naturally get compacted after watering the garden. I had to add some soil so that it rose above the wood. You can use a hose or the watering can to water the garden prior to planting the herbs.

Planning to create a medium-sized or larger garden? You should also consider water-saving watering methods, like a soaker hose.

Dig Holes In Your Garden

To do this, use the trowel to dig planting holes. The size of the planting holes should be about two inches in depth and two inches in diameter. The space between one hole and the other depends on the herbs you are planting.

If you have poor quality soil, consider using D.A.P fertilizer when planting. Mix a handful of the fertilizer with the soil in every hole.

Start from seed? Or transplant established greens?

You can get a great jump start on the growing season by starting seeds indoors in the perfect growing environment: a humid little indoor greenhouse sitting in the sunshine on your windowsill. You can begin to see growth in 5-14 days, and once the plants are more established, transplant them outdoors in a sunny spot. It's definitely easy to grow them yourself, and comparatively less expensive than buying individual plants ($2 for seeds vs. $10 for plants).

That said, there's nothing wrong with going to the store and hand-picking your baby plants. You can tell which plants are healthy and have a better chance of surviving the transplant, and you can also use the opportunity to explore your options and take in the fresh herbal scents. One of my favorite things to do is to compare all of the mint plants at the Rochester Public Market – there's a specialty vendor who brings 20+ varieties of mints, each yielding a different scent and flavor, such as banana mint, chocolate mint, strawberry mint, etc.

Plant Your Herbs

Transplant your herbs from the nursery to the garden. Water the nursery before transplanting so that it is easy to uproot the herbs without damaging their roots. When planting your herbs, place the young seedling upright into the hole and steady it by filling the soil on the sides. Water your seedlings after planting. Not sure on what herbs to plant? This glossary of commonly used herbs can be your starting point.

Consider the appeal of companion gardening

Companion gardening is a way to keep the peace in your garden, as plants are typically mutually beneficial of one another. Whether you're gardening herbs or a wider variety of fruits, vegetables and flowers, companion gardening as a general practice is important for a number of reasons:

When plants are located in close proximity, the nutrients in the soil are shared. Companion plants share the nutrients without inhibiting either plant's growth, whereas when plants demand the same type of nutrients, neither may reach their full potential.

Some plants create scents that ward off garden pests from attacking not only them, but the plants in their vicinity. Natural defense!

It's easy to plan your garden without considering how large the plants are going to be at full-size; if you're not cautious, some plants will completely sprawl and extinguish the sunlight from their shorter neighbors. Companion plants are less likely to overshadow one another, and even if one plant stands much taller, its counterpart might thrive well in its shade.

FIND A PLACE FOR YOUR HERB GARDEN

You have several choices when it comes to where you want to plant your herb garden. If you wish to go the more traditional route and place your herbs in an outdoor garden, make sure you choose a sunny space with full sun and rich soil, which will make an ideal place to plant your herb garden. But if your soil leaves much to be desired, you can certainly plant herbs in a raised garden bed and fill it with high-quality soil that your herbs need to thrive. If all your lawn space is in the shade, there are herbs, including parsley, mint and cilantro, that do well with just receiving 3 or 4 hours of sun. Rosemary, thyme and lavender would do better receiving more sun, so consider what the area you have in mind receives when it comes to sun and shade. You can simply check the plant tag to see how much sun each herb should receive.

It is important to note that if you live in a very hot climate, too much sun can dry out your herbs. This is another reason why planting your herbs in a container is a smart move because then you can move the container if you see they're receiving too much sun or shade.

If you have more space, a herb spiral could also work very well.

Balcony Herb Garden

A garden box attached to a balcony, filled with lavender, chives, rosemary and mint.

Many people might not have the outdoor space for a garden. Apartment buildings or condos often have no place for a personal garden. However, the absence of a lawn does not mean that you can't have a garden!

If you don't have lawn space, but happen to have a balcony, that will make a great space for a windowsill herb garden. That way you'll have easy access to your herbs while allowing them to get the sunlight that they need. Simply secure either a box to the balcony, which will allow good drainage, or opt to set several containers with herbs on the balcony.

Indoor Herb Garden

Many herbs can be grown indoors so if you don't have outdoor space or a balcony, you'll still be able to grow herbs indoors. Ideally, you may want to keep your herb garden in the kitchen so you can cook and bake and have quick and easy access to fresh, homegrown herbs.

To grow indoors, herbs need a lot of natural sunlight. We're talking at least six hours a day for most herbs. If your kitchen doesn't receive a lot of natural light or if you don't have the counter space there, you can absolutely set up your herb garden in another room.

Whatever room you decide, place your herb garden next to a window in a sunny spot. If you have a hard time finding a place that receives a lot of natural sun, you still have options! A grow light mimics direct sunlight so it can work if you can't find a sunny area in your home or apartment.

However, before purchasing a grow light, it might be worth it to see how your herbs so with the indoor sunlight that they're receiving. Watch for signs that your herbs aren't receiving enough sun, such as becoming pale in color and producing small leaves. If there's not enough sun inside or outside your home, you may want to look at getting a grow light.

As for temperature, herbs will be happy with a mild 65-70-degree indoor temperature.

Feeding Your Growing Herbs

It's important to plant your herbs in high-quality potting soil. Once your herbs are planted, you'll want to make you sure to regularly water these plants, especially in the summer months. If you choose to keep your herb garden outdoors, a good garden hose will help you easily water all your herbs and other plants while saving you time. We recommend the Reel RSH125 Crate Hose Reel for a high-quality self-winding hose that will help you well water your herbs and other plants without getting caught and tangled as you water.

As stated above, growing herbs are pretty easy to maintain as they typically don't require fertilizer, as long as you use a high-quality potting soil. Once again, be sure to check the plant tag well for the special needs of each herb.

CHAPTER THREE

How to Harvest Herbs From Your Herb Garden?

When it comes to harvesting your herbs, the more plants you pick, the more plants you will get so harvest often. It's also important to harvest before your herbs start flowering because you'll get more flavorful, better tasting herbs before the plants start to flower so make sure to check how much they're yielding.

Make sure not to remove more than one-third of the plant to ensure that it will keep growing. When harvesting, just pinch off individual leaves, not the whole stalk. Remember to pinch back after harvesting.

Whether you plan to use fresh herbs in a recipe, or dry them to use later, growing them yourself ensures that you'll have plenty or fresh, flavorful herbs ready at your fingertips.

CREATIVE DIY HERB GARDENS FOR INDOORS AND OUTDOORS

Regardless of whether you have a small garden, a huge garden or no garden at all, there should be no excuse for not growing your herbs. They're very easy to maintain and there truly is nothing better than picking your very own fresh herbs right in your home. You can build a big garden feature or a subtler indoor hanging garden or wall; either way, an herb garden won't only provide you with fresh produce and delicious food, but it'll also brighten up your home. And don't even get me started on the wonderful smells that will be emanating from your little plants!

Pallet herb planters

The reason why pallet projects are so amazing is that they offer endless possibilities to beautify your home, and the same rule applies when using them for indoor gardens.

Unlike what you think, pallet planters are easy to make, and even easier to personalize with the desired decorations.

Herbs planted in tea cans

Use your old tea cans to make amazing herb pots.

Herbs in wooden basket

This is one of our top suggestions for creating a centerpiece indoor garden, as long as you have an available wooden box to use as a container. One thing you must remember here is to combine plants with at least similar sun and water requirements.

Pegboard herb gardens

Pegboards' value consists exactly in their almost unrestricted versatility –
applying this solution, it will be easy to keep shears nearby planted in
adorable mugs, galvanized pails or small handmade pots.

Vintage herb planters

With the proper drainage in place, you can make planters from literally
everything. Just visit the closest thrift shop, and look for the prettiest vintage-
styled tines that would look nice on your windowsill.

HERB GARDENS HANGING FROM THE COFFEE TINS

There is hardly any inner garden that is easier to make – just select the herbs you want to plant, find a suitable location where you can reach for them and pluck them, and hang them on coffee tins.

Herbs planted in tea cups

Ever thought what to do with the amazing vintage tea set that is too old to drink from? Planting herbs inside is a wonderful idea, and will allow you to make the most beautiful garden you could have imagined.

Wall pockets made of durable fabrics

This is another simple and affordable DIY project for passionate homeowners that can be considered both in the kitchen and the other rooms around the house.

With fabrics, nevertheless, you must prevent water from dripping on the walls, and direct it towards the sink or the tub in the bathroom.

Herb gardens in kitchen utensils

There is no need to get rid of old utensils and metal boilers – they can easily become your brand new planters, and collate all herbs you need.

Herb gardens placed in drawers

We all have unused drawers lying in the garage for years, so why not using them to grow herbs? Put pots inside, align them in the desired way, and you're ready to go.

Bottle-top vertical herb gardens

This idea is both functional and stunningly beautiful, and gives you the chance to reuse large plastic bottles. All you need to do is to open their bottom for drainage, and see how their shape converts plants into wonderful mini trees.

Rolling herbs

The kitchen may be the perfect place for your herbs, but it won't always be the best lit room you have at home.

The best thing you can do to ensure plants have all sunlight they need is to put the pots on bar carts, and move them from one area to the other.

Mason Jar Garden

The Mason jar craze is still in full force, and I don't think it'll be dying down anytime soon. So when it comes to using them for DIY projects, making a wall herb garden just seems like the next logical step!

Without holes for drainage you have to be careful not to overwater your plants; you could also put some stones in the bottom of the jar so that the water sits there and not in the soil.

Herb Spiral

This spiral idea is absolutely stunning and will make for a wonderful feature in your garden; depending on how much space you have, you can make it as big or small as you like. With a raised garden bed design, your herbs will be safe from weeds and better protected from cold temperatures.

Faux Ladder Planter

I just love the ladder design of this planter – it just really suits the outdoors. You don't have to be a professional carpenter to pull off this relatively easy build, and the best part is that the whole thing won't cost you more than $50.

Simple Hanging Garden

This indoor hanging garden is the epitome of elegance; the minimalist design is what makes it so appealing. It won't take all that long to make this and you actually don't need that many supplies either. Just make sure to pick a spot in your home that gets enough sunlight.

Bottle-Top Vertical Garden

Not only is this project adorable and functional, but it's a great way to reuse those old plastic two-liter bottles. The opening at the bottom provides the necessary drainage, and the shape makes your herbs look like mini trees.

BENEFITS OF GROWING YOUR OWN DIY HERB GARDEN

Why should you go through all the trouble of growing your own herbs when there are plenty of fresh herbs for sale at the market? What's the point to getting all that dirt under your fingernails when you could pull open a plastic package and get the same ingredients? There's more to herb gardening than meets the eye, and the benefits are profound.

Fresh Herbs Always Available

One of the best benefits of growing your own herbs is having fresh herbs right at your fingertips, whenever you want or need them. When you have your own herb garden growing right outside — or inside — your door, you'll always have the right ingredients waiting for you to make dinner time magic.

No Boring Dinners

Adding a few different herbs to a simple chicken dinner makes it a whole new meal. Your simple side dishes become the main feature. Potatoes are a new adventure on a nightly basis. The results are only limited to the types of herbs you decide to plant and how daring you want to be with your menu.

Good For You

Adding fresh herbs to your diet is a great way to boost your meal's vitamin value, but that isn't the only health benefit you can obtain. Gardening is a wonderful form of exercise. All of that digging, bending, and stretching will pay off in tightly toned muscles, and if you keep at it, you'll also achieve a bit of weight loss and healthily glowing skin.

Save Money

Let's face it, fresh herbs can be expensive when you purchase them individually at the grocery store every time you need them, and the local grocer doesn't always stock all the herbs you are looking for. When this happens, you'll need to find a specialty store, where you are going to pay even more. After the initial investment of getting your herb garden started, the money you save will be your own.

Educational

Herb gardening is an educational experience for adults as well as for children. There is always something new to learn, whether it be a new gardening technique, a different recipe, a new and improved use for the herbs you thought you knew so well, or the fascinating history of herbs that dates way back to medieval times.

Relieve Stress

Tending, or just visiting an herb garden can do a world of good towards relieving all that built up stress that daily life likes to give us. The sights and scents that abound in an herb garden delight the senses and revitalize the soul. Having one at your own home makes it that much easier.

Curb Appeal

Adding an herb garden to your home's landscape gives your yard real curb appeal. Most herbs are just as pretty as shrubs and flowers. You can even add them to your shrubs and flowers if you don't have room for a formal herb garden. They blend in beautifully.

Share the Wealth

Growing your own herbs means that you'll always have more than enough herbs than you can possibly use, leaving you plenty of extras to share with friends, family, and neighbors. Just think how popular you will be when you show up at the next dinner invite with a basket full of fresh herbs. Dried fresh herbs in pretty jars make wonderful gifts too!

Exotic Variety

Did you know that there are more than 30 different types of basil? The local market will usually only carry the most common, sweet basil. Dark opal basil, which is purple in color, is a bit more difficult to find, as are cinnamon basil, anise basil, Italian basil, and globe basil, which happens to be perfect for those of you with smaller gardens. Growing your own herb garden will allow you to sample some of the other more exotic and fun herbs that are out there waiting for you.

Good Clean Fun

Okay, well maybe it's not the cleanest hobby, but gardening and watching your fresh herbs grow is well worth the little bit of dirt you'll need to wash off. Get out there and start planning your own beautiful and aromatic herb garden. It really is fun, and the benefits can't be beat.

ADVANTAGES OF DIY HERB GARDEN

Herbs year round.

An indoor herb garden gives the gardeners afflicted with winter malaise an opportunity to lovingly tend to more plants and enjoy herbs year round after the outdoor growing season has ended.

Low maintenance.

Many herbs are relatively low maintenance to grow, all it takes is being mindful of the minimal watering and lighting requirements for each. Some really easy-to-grow options include lemongrass, chives, mint, and parsley.

Save money.

One of the best benefits of growing herbs indoors is the cost savings. You can grow your own herbs for the fraction of the cost you spend on them at the supermarket or farmer's market. The cost of fresh basil, for example, can be $2-3 (possibly more depending where you are located) for a few ounces. The cost of a packet of basil seeds is only a dollar or two and, if you nurture your plants, will yield you a bounty of fresh herbs on a weekly basis for a very long time.

They're truly fresh.

When you snip off herbs in your indoor herb garden, you know they are the freshest they can possibly be. How long do you think the herbs at your grocery store have been sitting there? The answer is 'a while.'

They're a healthy option.

It is possible to boost the flavor of your everyday meals without adding fat, sodium or sugar. Fresh herbs are a great low-calorie and delicious way to add zest and flair to your cuisine, making this one of the most compelling indoor herb gardening pros. When you cook with fresh herbs, your dishes will never be bland or boring.

They're pleasing to the senses.

Herbs are edible but are also ornamental and will definitely add an element of interest to your existing décor with their various foliage colors and shapes. And, in some cases, there are aromatic herbs whose foliage gives off a nice fragrance.

DISADVANTAGES OF DIY HERBS GARDEN

Herbs require lots of light.

Most all herb plants require at least 6-8 hours of sunlight to thrive. While outside this isn't normally an issue, indoors is quite another story. The average home may not have sufficient light, making the likelihood of your plants' survival hanging in the balance. The best lighting can be found in a south-facing window, but not all homes have this option, which leaves the only other option as supplemental grow lights. Leggy plants is a good sign that those herbs need more sunlight.

Additional lighting can be costly.

For those having little light and in need of more, this is simply another added cost to growing herbs in the home. While it may not be a steep expense depending on the type of lighting you get and for how many plants, it's still something to be considered and factored in before considering that indoor herb garden.

Warm temps are important.

It's no secret that most herbs like heat. In fact, many are native to warm regions. That said, indoor heat during winter can be quite dry and not exactly the best for thriving herb plants. While you can spend time misting your plants to keep them from drying out or even set them on a water-filled tray of pebbles to improve humidity, this can lead to additional problems if you're not careful.

Watering can be tricky.

As you mist your plants to keep their foliage moist and lush, water becomes yet another issue with indoor herb gardening. First, if you have high sodium content or your water is treated with chemicals, this could ultimately be harmful to plants. And as most herbs prefer drier conditions; unfortunately, we tend to kill our plants with kindness, especially in winter. Too much of a good thing really is, as too much water can be detrimental, leading to root rot and the eventual demise of your much beloved plants.

Better double check for bugs.

While you're busy watering, you'll have to be on the lookout for pests that may be hiding in the plants, like aphids or spider mites, especially when potted plants are brought indoors from outside. Others may be attracted to the soil, as is the case with fungus gnats.